STATE PATROL

by Patrick Nau

Carolrhoda Books, Inc., Minneapolis

Thanks to the Minnesota State Patrol, especially
to Floyd (Bud) Hanson. Without your help this
book could not have been written.

LIBRARY OF CONGRESS CATALOGING IN PUBLICATION DATA

Nau, Patrick.
  State patrol.

  Summary: Describes the work of the state patrol with
emphasis on the duties of the troopers, cooperation with
local police departments, the structure and activities of
the headquarters, and many other aspects.
  1. Police, State–United States–Juvenile literature.
[1. Police, State] I. Title.
HV8138.N357 1984   363.2'0973   83-27216
ISBN 0-87614-264-1 (lib. bdg.)

1 2 3 4 5 6 7 8 9 10 93 92 91 90 89 88 87 86 85 84

For Dennis and Rita, who have helped me
above and beyond the call of duty.
Thanks for everything.

Every state in the United States except for Hawaii has a state patrol. In some states it may be called the State Highway Patrol, in others the State Police, but whatever it is called, each state patrol works to make our lives safer.

The men and women who work for the state patrol are often called state troopers. Some states have large forces of troopers. California, for example, has over 5,000. Other forces are relatively small, like North Dakota's force of 98. Most lie somewhere in between, like Minnesota's force of 507.

Whether or not you have noticed them, you have probably seen your state patrol at work. You may have been traveling on a highway and passed a trooper helping someone whose car had broken down. Perhaps you have passed an accident and seen a trooper directing traffic or giving first aid. Or you may have been a passenger in a car that was speeding, and a trooper pulled the car over and issued the driver a traffic ticket.

The main duty of most state patrols is to enforce highway and motor vehicle laws. State police may have additional duties as well. The state patrol shown in this book has three primary responsibilities: dealing with accidents, providing assistance to motorists, and enforcing traffic laws. In addition, the state patrol does many other things that most people don't see or even know about.

A section of the control panel in the control room

Most states are divided into several state patrol districts. The district headquarters is the communications center for that district.

Each district is divided into smaller units called stations. Station offices are usually located in local police stations.

At the heart of the district headquarters is the control room, where calls are received and messages are dispatched (delivered over a two-way radio) to troopers. Every year the state patrol receives thousands of calls for help. In addition, the control room is linked by radio to all local police and sheriffs' departments. Every call that comes into the control room is recorded, and the tape is kept for 24 hours in case someone needs to listen to a call again later.

Each district receives up-to-date weather reports so that it can prepare for bad weather if necessary.

The dispatcher speaks to a trooper from the control room at district headquarters.

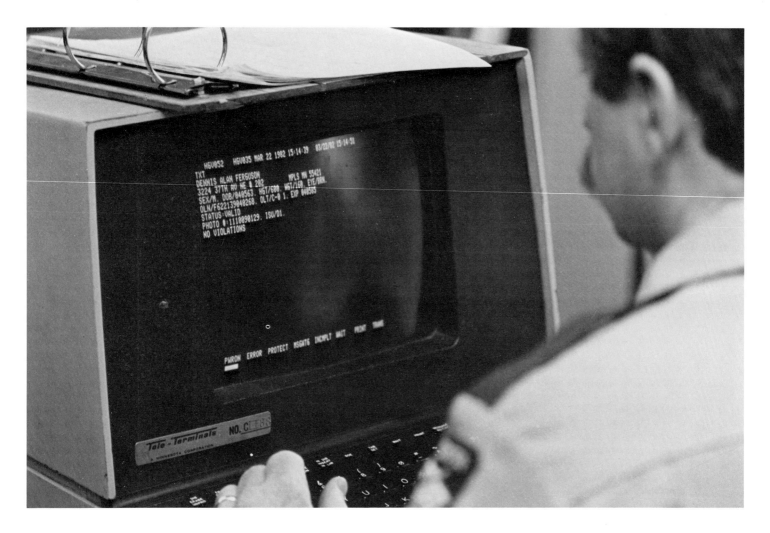

The control room is equipped with a computer that can check on drivers' licenses and license plates and provide information about motorists who have been stopped. If the motorist is wanted for any crimes, is AWOL (away without leave) from the armed service, or has been reported missing, this information will appear on the computer screen. The computer also prints out FBI bulletins about criminals thought to be in the state.

The control room has direct communications links with national law enforcement agencies. For example, if the president were coming to your state, the Secret Service would be in contact with your state patrol to help provide the president with proper security.

Television screens showing freeway entrance ramps

The state patrol works closely with the state Department of Transportation (often called the DOT for short). In some states the DOT operates a traffic management center. These centers are equipped with television screens on which freeway entrance ramps can be watched. If there is a problem on a ramp, a dispatcher from the center reports it immediately to the state patrol.

The state patrol and the DOT also operate a 24-hour-a-day public information telephone service. Travelers can call in to find out road conditions, such as detours, road construction, or weather conditions, on the routes they plan to travel.

The district headquarters and the DOT are connected by a direct telephone line so that events such as traffic emergencies or power outages can be reported and acted on immediately.

Most state troopers do not spend much time at their district headquarters. Their "offices" are in their cars. Each trooper is assigned to a specific section of highway, sometimes called a beat. The number of troopers assigned to each beat depends on the size and highway activity of the beat.

Beats are patrolled in three 8-hour shifts. In metropolitan areas, highways are patrolled 24 hours a day. In most outlying areas there is no third shift. Troopers getting off the second shift are "on call" until the morning shift begins. If a call comes into district headquarters in the middle of the night, it is dispatched to a trooper at home.

Troopers drive their cars home after their work shifts are over. When their next work shifts begin, they radio headquarters and check in as soon as they enter their cars. From that moment, each trooper is on duty.

Troopers are responsible for the upkeep of
their patrol cars.

Troopers carry everything they need to
do their jobs with them in their cars.

 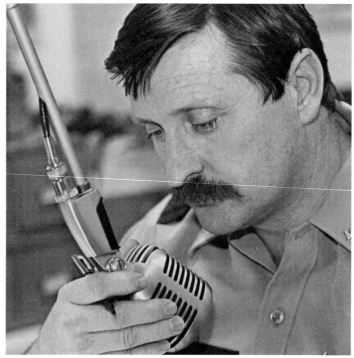

Whenever a trooper plans to leave the patrol car for any length of time and so will be away from the car's two-way radio, the trooper must radio headquarters with his or her location. The trooper pictured above is about to take a lunch break. She is calling headquarters with the restaurant's name and phone number so that she can be contacted immediately in case there is an emergency. As soon as she is back in her car, she will radio headquarters that she is back on duty.

So that there will be no misunderstandings between the troopers and the dispatcher at headquarters, the state patrol uses a number code when talking over the radio. A dispatcher who wishes to contact a specific trooper might say, "SP 416 Valley." SP stands for state patrol, 416 is the trooper's badge number, and Valley is the name of the district headquarters. The trooper being called responds by saying "10-4," which means that the message is being received loud and clear. The dispatcher might continue by saying, "There is a 10-52 at the river junction." A 10-52 is a personal injury accident. Every kind of crime or emergency has its own number. For example, 10-54 indicates a death.

A trooper asks to see a motorist's driver's license.

Not all of a trooper's work is dispatched from headquarters, though. Since troopers average roughly 75% of their working time patrolling in their cars, they come across many situations that headquarters knows nothing about. Troopers deal with these situations as they come up.

Because a beat often covers many miles, there may be several troopers patrolling it at the same time. They keep in touch with one another by two-way radio. In many instances more than one trooper will respond to a call for help. The first trooper to arrive at the scene of an accident or other emergency is in charge.

When a trooper stops a motorist for a driving violation like speeding, the first thing the trooper does is ask to see the motorist's driver's license.

Then the trooper radios the dispatcher at headquarters for a license check. The trooper tells the dispatcher the driver's name, driver's license number, and license plate number, and the dispatcher punches this information into the computer. The motorist's driving record, to whom the car is registered, whether or not the driver's license is valid, and any other important information about the driver will appear on the computer screen. The dispatcher then relays this information to the trooper.

If everything checks out, the trooper will simply give the driver a traffic ticket. If, on the other hand, the motorist's license is not valid, the trooper will issue a citation. The driver will then have to appear in court. If the computer has indicated that the driver is wanted for a crime or the car is a stolen vehicle, the trooper will arrest the driver and bring him or her to the nearest police station or sheriff's office.

A driver who has been issued a traffic ticket can either pay the fine or, if he believes he is innocent, request a court hearing. As soon as the driver either pays the fine or is found guilty by the court, the violation is added to the other information about this driver that is stored in the computer.

14

Cars that have been left unoccupied along the roadsides are common occurrences. When a trooper comes across one of these vehicles, he or she will stop to check it. After running a license plate check, the trooper will fasten a bright orange tag to the antenna or windshield wipers. Written on the tag is the exact time the car was checked by the trooper. If the car hasn't been moved within the next four hours, it will be towed away. The tag also tells other troopers who pass by that the car has already been checked and they don't need to stop.

If the driver is still with the vehicle, possibly trying to fix it, the trooper will stop and offer assistance. The trooper will park the patrol car, with lights flashing, behind the stalled vehicle, never in front of it. This protects the stalled car from being hit from behind.

Many motorists are good at fixing car problems and don't need any help. Others may need a tow truck, a ride to the nearest gas station, or some water for an overheated radiator.

Sometimes a vehicle stalls or runs out of gas in the middle of a busy highway, and the driver is unable to move it to the side of the road. This can be a very dangerous situation. The trooper on the scene will use the patrol car, which is equipped with specially designed bumpers, to push the car or truck to a safe area where it can be worked on or towed away.

Anytime a trooper offers assistance to a motorist, such as calling for a tow truck or giving directions, that assistance must be noted on an "aid sheet." The state patrol uses a computer to evaluate these aid sheets, find out where troopers are giving the most assistance, and pinpoint problem areas.

After making sure that the situation is under control, the trooper fills in the aid sheet and begins patrolling again.

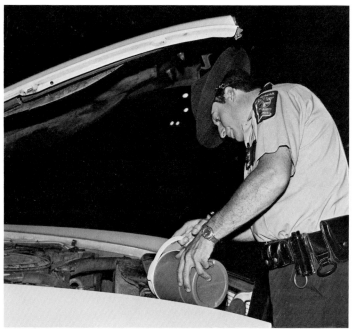

Another major responsibility of the state patrol is the investigation and reporting of traffic accidents. When a trooper arrives at the scene of a major accident, he or she follows a specific procedure. First, the patrol car must be parked so that it will prevent further accidents. Next, the trooper must check for injuries, give first aid, and radio for an ambulance and/or a fire truck if necessary.

Then the trooper must check for dangerous situations, such as a leaking gas tank that could cause a fire. The trooper's next task is to gather witnesses and try to determine what caused the accident. The trooper also checks to see if any of the drivers involved are intoxicated. Finally the trooper fills out an official accident report.

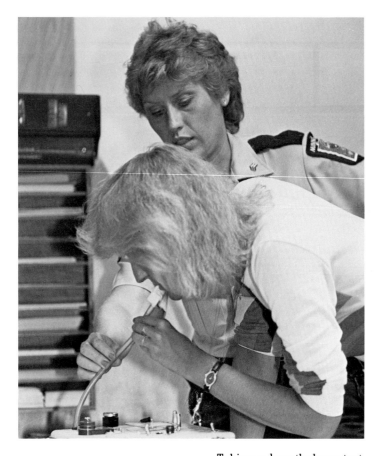

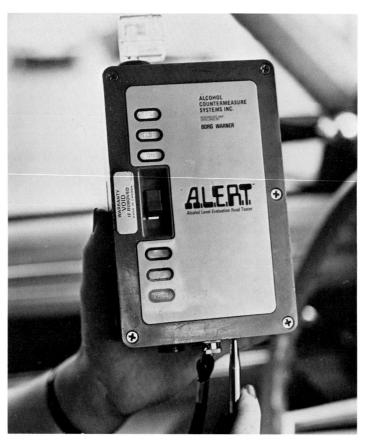

Taking a breathalyser test

A portable breath tester

One of the major goals of the state patrol is the apprehension of drunk drivers. Drunk drivers kill and injure thousands of people every year. When a trooper observes a motorist who is driving dangerously, he or she will pull the motorist over and run a license check. By talking to and observing the driver, the trooper can determine whether or not the driver appears drunk. If so, the driver will be asked to take a breath test on the portable breath tester, usually called the PBT. If the test is positive, the motorist may be arrested and taken to the nearest police station or sheriff's office. There the driver will be given another test on a machine called a breathalyser. The breathalyser test can be used as evidence in court. If this test is positive, the driver will be charged with driving while intoxicated and possibly jailed.

Troopers are often called on to testify in court about traffic tickets, accidents, or drunk driving cases that have come to trial. They must keep accurate information when making arrests so that they can recall all the facts if they are called on to testify later.

Troopers have the authority to shut down highways in an emergency. Sometimes a trooper will be called on to locate a person traveling on the road. There may be an emergency in the person's family or the person may have been reported as a runaway.

This patrolman is talking with an illegal hitchhiker to determine whether or not he is also a runaway.

Sometimes a local community police department may be faced with a problem too large or widespread for it to handle. The state patrol will help out when asked. Some state patrols have special vehicles called mobile communications vans that are equipped with complete communications facilities. The van can be sent to the trouble spot where it will be used as a command post for the troopers helping out.

State troopers have the power to make arrests throughout the state for offenses committed in their presence. Local police departments can usually make arrests only in their own districts.

The state patrol has personnel who do not patrol in cars but who perform special public services instead. One such service is the school bus inspection program. All school buses in the state are given a thorough inspection once a year.

This state trooper is stationed at the entrance to the governor's mansion.
All guests must receive clearance to come inside.

Another service is the provision of around-the-clock security for the governor and his or her family. The state patrol also provides security for the state legislature when it is in session.

Yet another responsibility of the state patrol is the enforcement of highway weight laws. The patrol operates both permanent and portable weigh stations throughout the state to weigh large trucks. Truck drivers or companies whose trucks carry more than the legal weight limit are fined. Overweight trucks cause major damage to our roadways every year.

Two special functions of the state patrol involve elementary schools. They are the bicycle safety program and the school patrol program. In the bicycle safety program, troopers visit schools throughout the state to talk with children about bicycle safety. The state patrol also checks on school patrols, encouraging them to do a good, safe job at street crossings.

A state patrol pilot goes over a map with a trooper to determine which area he should cover next during a search and rescue operation.

A view of a highway from the air

Many state patrols have aircraft systems. This state's aircraft system averages over 4,000 hours in the air each year. Its duties include search and rescue operations, criminal surveillance, crime-scene photography, and traffic monitoring. A pilot can clock a speeder from the air and radio a trooper on the ground to issue the speeding motorist a traffic ticket. The patrol uses both airplanes and helicopters when operating searches, such as looking for children lost in the woods, trailing bank robbers, or looking for plane crashes.

The duties of state patrols and state police vary somewhat from state to state. The major difference is that usually the duties of state patrols are more limited than those of state police. The main duty of most patrols, such as those in California or Minnesota, is to enforce highway and motor vehicle laws. State police forces, such as those in New York and New Mexico, share that duty but are also responsible for general police work such as criminal investigations. Vermont is unusual in that its state police force is larger than any other law enforcement agency in the state and provides basic police services to many small communities. This is because there are no large cities or metropolitan areas in Vermont.

Whether you have a state police force in your state or a state patrol, its duties are likely to include most of the things mentioned in this book. There may be minor differences. California, for example, does not consider providing weather and road condition information a primary duty of its state patrol. New Mexico, on the other hand, does. Some states don't have aircraft systems. Others may operate by procedures that are a little different. But although *your* state patrol may not operate *exactly* as the one shown in this book, many of its basic responsibilities and procedures are probably the same.